POP CHARTS

100 ICONIC SONG LYRICS VISUALIZED

———

KATRINA McHUGH

HARPER
DESIGN

An Imprint of HarperCollinsPublishers

The Anatomy of a Pop Chart

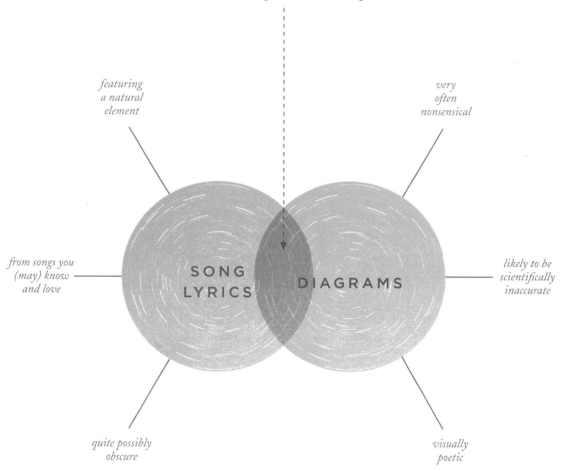

featuring
a natural
element

very
often
nonsensical

from songs you
(may) know
and love

SONG LYRICS

DIAGRAMS

likely to be
scientifically
inaccurate

quite possibly
obscure

visually
poetic

Start
Here

INTRODUCTION

Music brings us together. It helps us feel alive. It speaks for us when, left to our own clumsy devices, we can't seem to find the right words. We save it for the moments that matter most. We get lost in it on headphones. We look to it for distraction, wisdom, meaning, escape. It makes us fling our bodies around. It lulls us to sleep. It can mend or break our hearts. Throughout our lives a vast catalog of random popular song lyrics clangs around in our collective subconscious, a wonderful hodgepodge language of inconsistent metaphors and cultural references tying us together. In seldom and often strange, extraordinary moments this can reveal itself. Like that night you braved karaoke, and strangers at the bar knew all the words and sang along.

This book is a celebration of those moments.

A few years ago, I found myself itching to slow down and reconnect creatively. Launching our design studio, Flight Design Co., had been all-consuming and I found myself daydreaming about simple things I had loved to do when I was younger, like excitedly tearing the plastic sleeve off a new album and, as it played, reading along with its liner notes in their entirety. Serendipitously, I discovered Elle Luna's global art event, the "100-Day Project," and on a whim elected to participate by diagramming pop song lyrics. As I began to listen more closely, I realized even the most cliché of songs can read like poetry, offering an insight and story (or at the very least, a good laugh, as was my personal case with Meatloaf's "Bat Out of Hell"[1]). The more I listened, the more I heard recurring themes in some of my favorites. The wind. The moon. Rivers and valleys. Countless allusions to the world around us.

Seizing on this connection, I began to create art prints that combined song lyrics with elements of nature (sharing them under the name *100 Days of Lyrical Natural Sciences*). I gave myself these rules: anything related to an observed natural phenomenon, an animal, leaves, rocks, outer space, the stars, et cetera would play. I envisioned creating a quirky infographic encyclopedia where nature and song lyrics would, sometimes illogically, collide and play off each other. As I listened to popular songs, I focused on the tiny natural details. From "don't go chasing waterfalls"[2] to "a hard rain's a-gonna fall,"[3] the variations felt endless, as did the sometimes silly nuggets of pop wisdom contained therein. I began drawing inspiration from the bright and shiny bits and pieces around me: a good friend sharing a song, my old sketchbooks filled with haphazard drawings of flora and fauna, a vintage set of encyclopedias inherited from my grandfather, an old journal of my great-grandmother's in which she transcribed *Le Langage des Fleurs* in perfect, flowing penmanship—the allusions were poetic. An acacia given to a lover or friend signaled pure, platonic love. An anemone signaled abandon.

For as long as songs have brought us together, songwriters have been drawing from nature to convey messages. We may not quite have the right words for big ideas like love, but a timeless phrase like "sunshine of my life"[4] feels solid and relatable. Natural elements have been woven into songs since songs have

[1] *Figure 82, "Bat Out of Hell" by Meatloaf*
[2] *Figure 2, "Waterfalls" by TLC*
[3] *Figure 36, "A Hard Rain's A-Gonna Fall" by Bob Dylan*
[4] *Figure 19, "You Are the Sunshine of My Life" by Stevie Wonder*

Acacia
(LOVE)

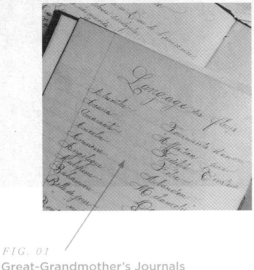

Great-Grandmother's Journals
"Language of Flowers," 1909

Grandfather's Encyclopedias
"Diagram of Photosynthesis," 1956

existed, and the powerful metaphors they supply us endure. The recurring signs and symbols don't have consistent meanings or translations, but nevertheless we forge onward, haphazardly borrowing from them to chart our emotional course. The moon represents a warm and romantic *saudade* in Neil Young's "Harvest Moon,"[5] but is linked with imminent disaster in "Bad Moon Rising"[6] by Creedence Clearwater Revival. Meanwhile, Astrud Gilberto's "Fly Me to the Moon"[7] portrays the moon as a magical and dreamy place where quite a lot of kissing happens. Basically, the meanings are all over the map—a realization that was driven home as I played with assigning shapes and symbols within each diagram.

[5] Figure 56, "Harvest Moon" by Neil Young
[6] Figure 59, "Bad Moon Rising" by Creedence Clearwater Revival
[7] Figure 73, "Fly Me to the Moon" by Astrud Gilberto

This was one of the first projects I'd embarked on in over a decade that truly had no client other than myself. It allowed me to play and reconnect with what led me toward a career in design in the first place, taking me back to that sweet teenage time when I would lie around with a friend having listening parties, poring over liner notes, drawing in our sketchbooks (or more rebelliously on the wall), and hopelessly trying to sort this weird world out. In sharing the images online I realized I wasn't alone in wanting a bit more of this in my life. I received messages from strangers about certain songs: one made them laugh, one was their wedding song. Occasionally, a follower would respond that they had never realized the lyrics before. "Wait a minute, all this time the words have been 'sweet dreams are made of *this*'"[8]? As simple as it may sound, in the end, letting go and creating something only for myself became the thing that connected me with others.

Following are one hundred "not-so-scientific" diagrams, each an homage to a song lyric (see The Anatomy of a Pop Chart on page 2). I offer them as a reminder to listen closely and to appreciate those moments that connect you to others across distance, culture, and time. For those of you who can guess a song without seeing the answers, well, we share a little secret.

Connection
(BRIEF, FLEETING)

[8] *Figure 95, "Sweet Dreams (Are Made of This)" by Eurythmics*

POP CHARTS

Figures 1–100

———

CAN YOU NAME THAT TUNE?

Each figure contains a sometimes rather secretive
homage to a particular pop song. Song name and artist
can be found on the back of each page.

Fig. 01

What I Compare You To

(T H E G R E Y)

(from)

Rose

KISS

Figure 01

"Kiss From a Rose"

Seal

Waterfalls ⟶

CHASING

Fig.
02

Stick to: ☑ **Rivers**
☑ **Lakes**
☐ **Ponds**

Figure 02

"Waterfalls"

TLC

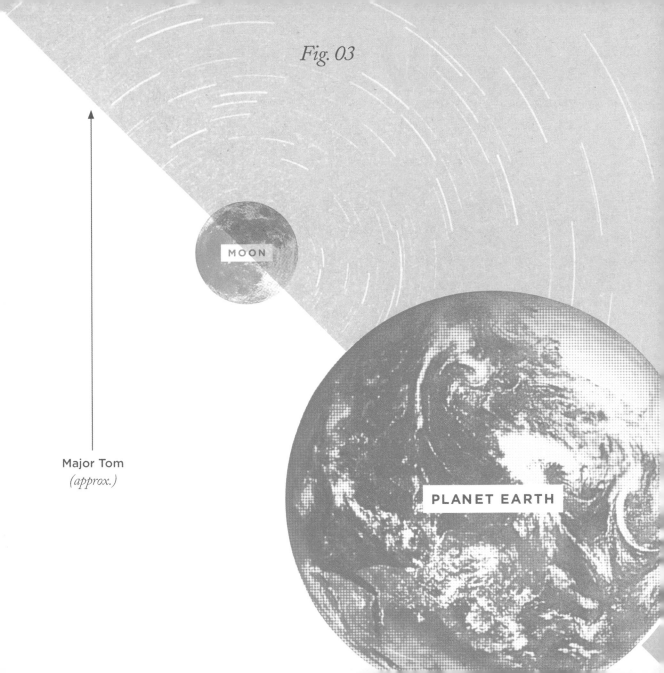

Fig. 03

MOON

PLANET EARTH

Major Tom
(approx.)

Figure 03

"Space Oddity"

David Bowie

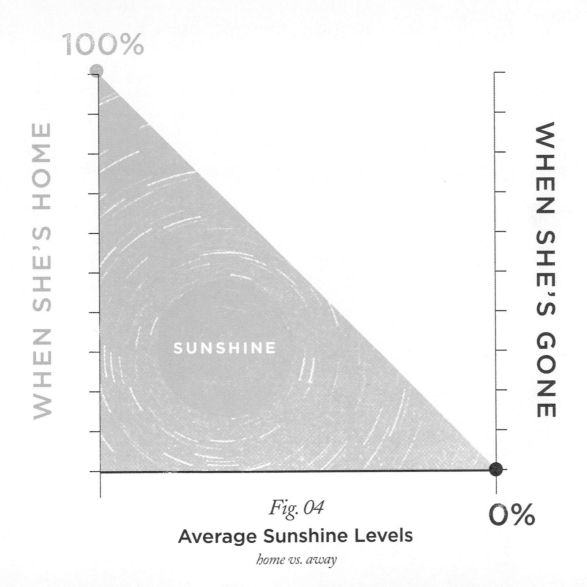

100%

WHEN SHE'S HOME

WHEN SHE'S GONE

SUNSHINE

0%

Fig. 04
Average Sunshine Levels
home vs. away

Figure 04

"Ain't No Sunshine"

Bill Withers

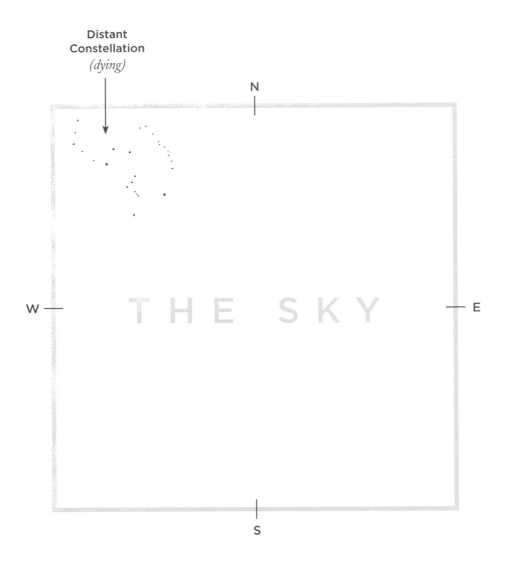

Fig. 05

Days of Miracle and Wonder

Figure 05

"The Boy in the Bubble"

Paul Simon

Fig. 06

NOT HIGH ENOUGH

A. **Mountain**

NOT LOW ENOUGH

B. **Valley**

DEFINITELY NOT WIDE ENOUGH

C. **River**

Figure 06

"Ain't No Mountain High Enough"

Marvin Gaye

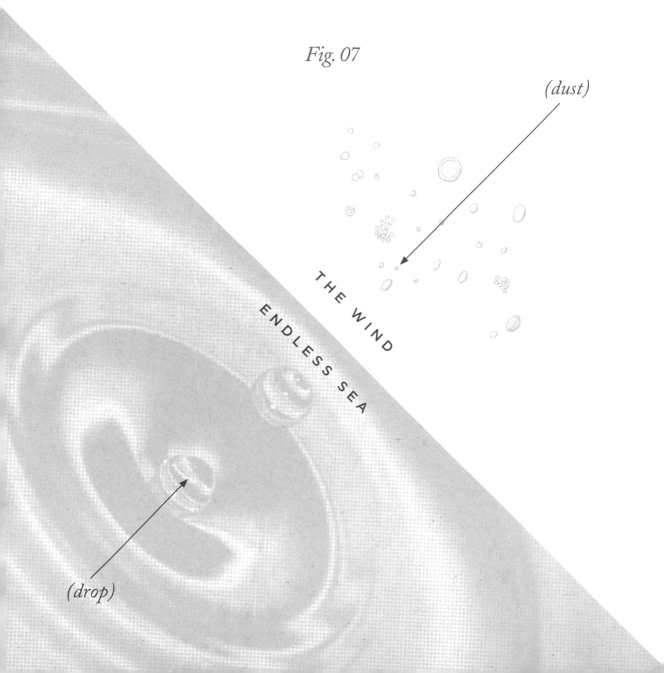

Fig. 07

(dust)

THE WIND

ENDLESS SEA

(drop)

Figure 07

"Dust in the Wind"
Kansas

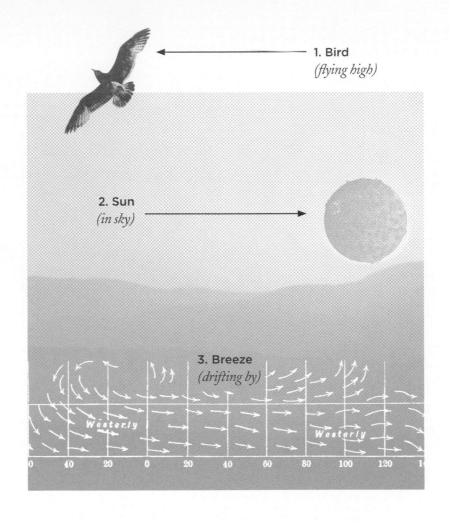

1. Bird
(flying high)

2. Sun
(in sky)

3. Breeze
(drifting by)

Fig. 08
Things That Know How I Feel

Figure 08

"Feeling Good"

Nina Simone

A. Where I Was Born
B. What I've Been Doing (Ever Since)

Fig.
09

A.

TENT
(little)

B. *RUNNING*

R I V E R

Figure 09

"A Change Is Gonna Come"

Sam Cooke

Fig. 10

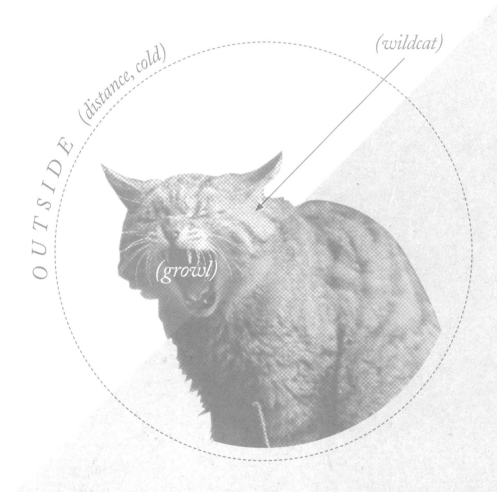

OUTSIDE *(distance, cold)*

(wildcat)

(growl)

Figure 10

"All Along the Watchtower"

Jimi Hendrix

Fig. 11

Where I Feel As One

THE
SUN
(in)

Figure 11

"All Apologies"

Nirvana

Fig. 12

What I Have Seen

1.) **Fire**   *2.)* **Rain**   *3.)* **Sunny Days**
                                        (never ending)

Figure 12

"Fire and Rain"

James Taylor

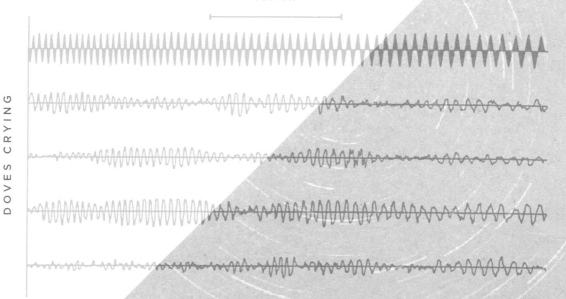

Fig.

13

DOVES CRYING

sound

Figure 13

"When Doves Cry"

Prince

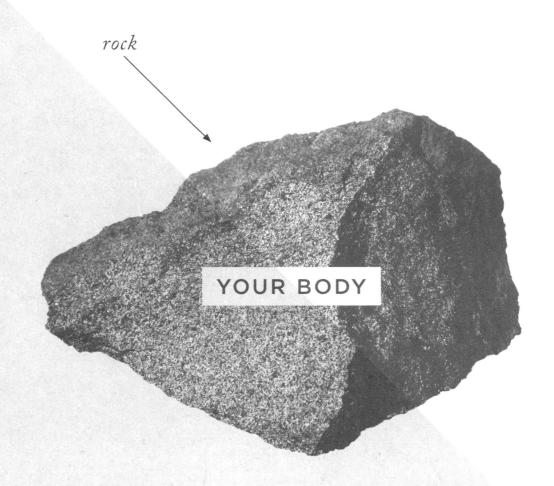

rock

YOUR BODY

Fig. 14
What I Will Do If You Stay

Figure 14

"Rock Your Body"

Justin Timberlake

Fig. 15
What Is in Tune

THE
MOON
THE
SUN

EVERYTHING

(under sun)

Figure 15

"Eclipse"

Pink Floyd

Fig. 16
Water Running Dryness Level

DANGER!

(what we should not wait for)

Figure 16

"Water Runs Dry"

Boyz II Men

HEART*

EYES
(lying)

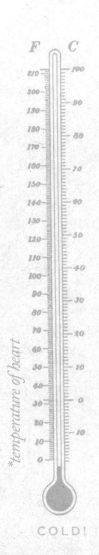

F   C

*temperature of heart

COLD!

Fig. 17

What He Is

Figure 17

"Cold Hearted"

Paula Abdul

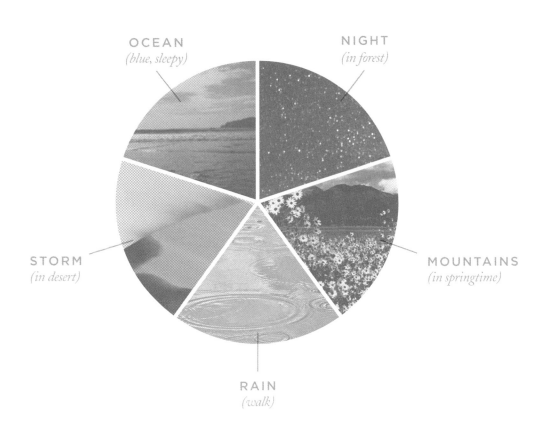

Fig. 18
My Senses

OCEAN
(blue, sleepy)

NIGHT
(in forest)

STORM
(in desert)

MOUNTAINS
(in springtime)

RAIN
(walk)

(1 0 0 %   F U L L)

Figure 18

"Annie's Song"

John Denver

Fig. 19

Reason I Will Always Stay Around

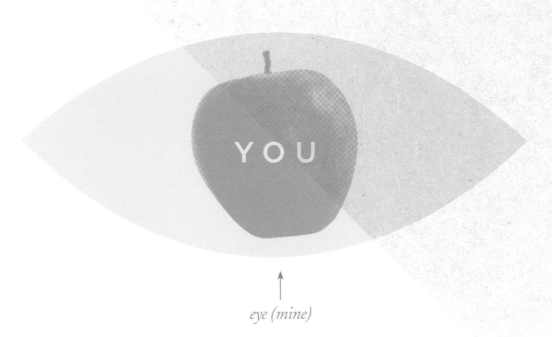

YOU

eye (mine)

Figure 19

"You Are the Sunshine of My Life"

Stevie Wonder

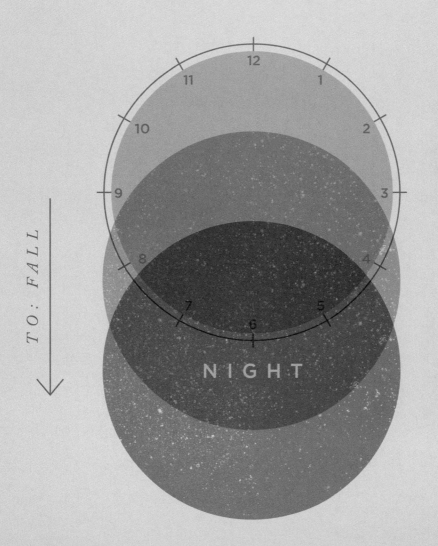

Fig. 20
What I'm Waiting For

TO: FALL

NIGHT

Figure 20

"Waiting for the Night"

Depeche Mode

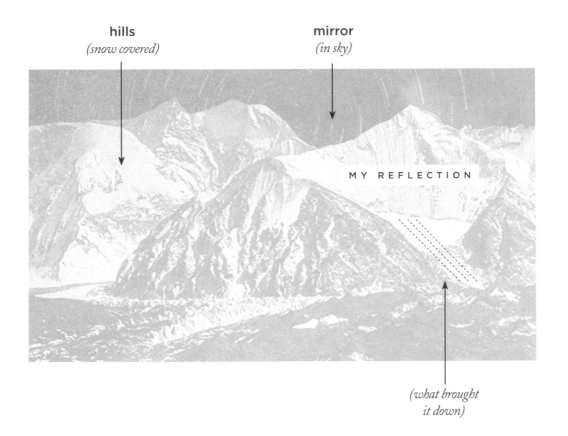

hills
(snow covered)

mirror
(in sky)

MY REFLECTION

*(what brought
it down)*

Fig. 21

Figure 21

"Landslide"

Fleetwood Mac

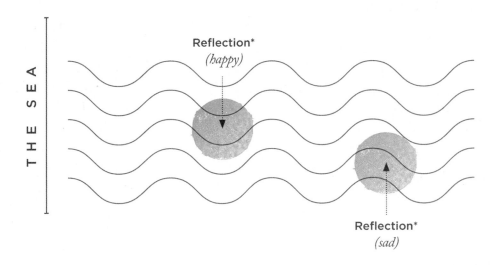

Fig. 22
What I Look To

Figure 22

"Come Sail Away"

Styx

Fig. 23
What the Shark Has

Teeth
pearly white

Figure 23

"Mack the Knife"

Louis Armstrong

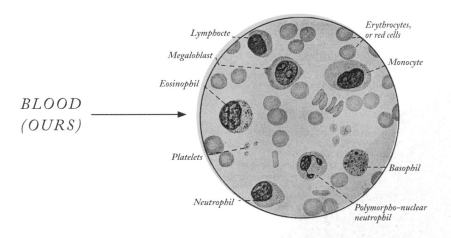

Lymphocte

Megaloblast

Eosinophil

Erythrocytes,
or red cells

Monocyte

**BLOOD
(OURS)**

Platelets

Basophil

Neutrophil

Polymorpho-nuclear
neutrophil

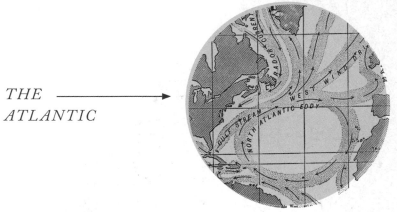

**THE
ATLANTIC**

Fig. 24
**Where Animals
Are Swimming**

Figure 24

"Third Planet"

Modest Mouse

Fig. 25

The Age That Is Dawning

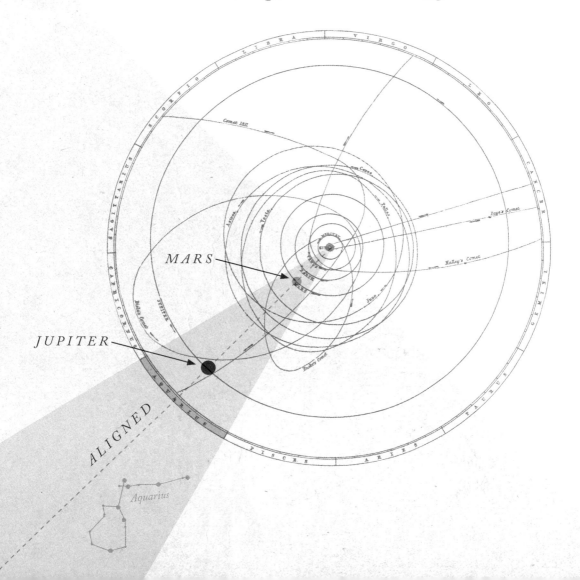

Figure 25

"Aquarius/Let the Sunshine In"

The 5th Dimension

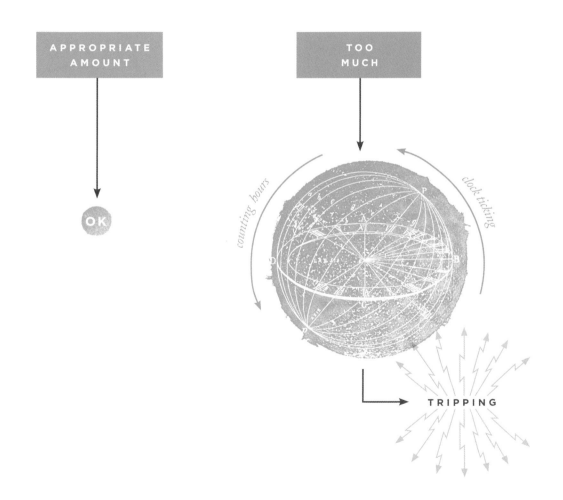

Fig. 26
Amount of Power per Man

Figure 26

"Power"

Kanye West

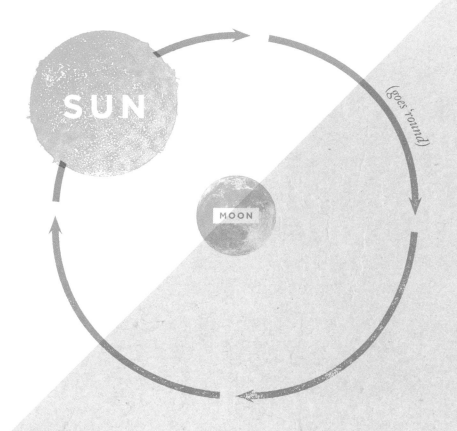

SUN

MOON

(goes 'round)

Fig. 27

What Happens Sometimes

Figure 27

"Save the Best for Last"

Vanessa Williams

(y)
B I R D

(x) W I R E

Fig.

28

How I Have Tried to Be Free
(in my way)

Figure 28

"Bird on the Wire"

Leonard Cohen

Fig. 29

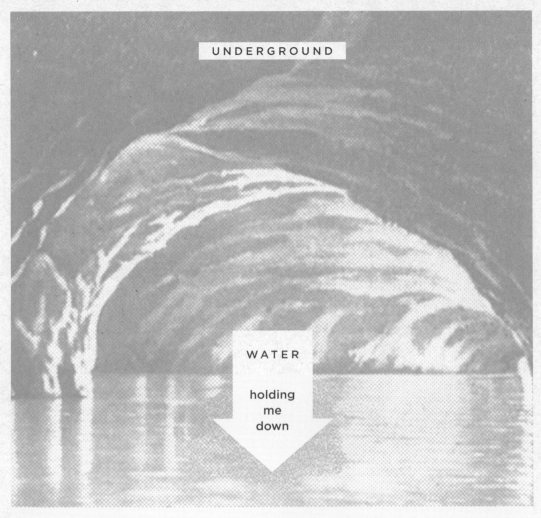

Figure 29

"Once in a Lifetime"

Talking Heads

Fig. 30
What Happened Before You Came

MY ROOM

Tornado

Mess Made
(please excuse it)

MOVING AIR

Figure 30

"Thinkin Bout You"

Frank Ocean

Fig. 31

Where You Will Find Me
(someday)

landslide

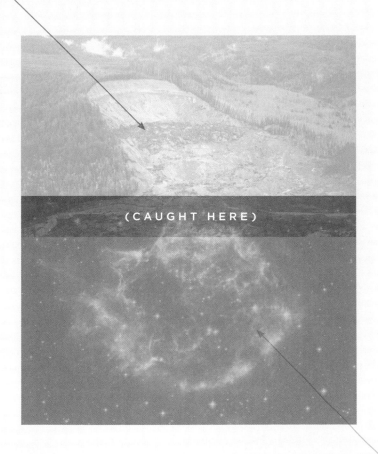

(CAUGHT HERE)

supernova

Figure 31

"Champagne Supernova"

Oasis

Fig.
32

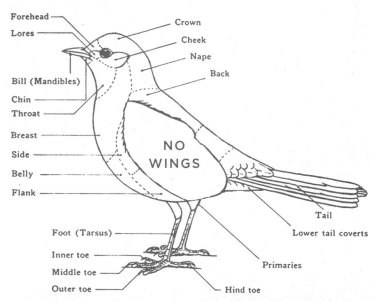

Scapulars
Lesser wing coverts
Middle wing coverts
Greater wing coverts
Tertials
Secondaries
Primaries

I would fly.

Forehead
Lores
Bill (Mandibles)
Chin
Throat
Breast
Side
Belly
Flank

Crown
Cheek
Nape
Back

NO WINGS

Tail
Lower tail coverts

Foot (Tarsus)
Inner toe
Middle toe
Outer toe

Primaries
Hind toe

CONTEMPLATING

Figure 32

"Regulate"

Warren G

Fig. 33

Not a Place to Raise Kids

MARS

Warm

Cold

Very Cold

Cold As Hell

Population:
0

Figure 33

"Rocket Man"

Elton John

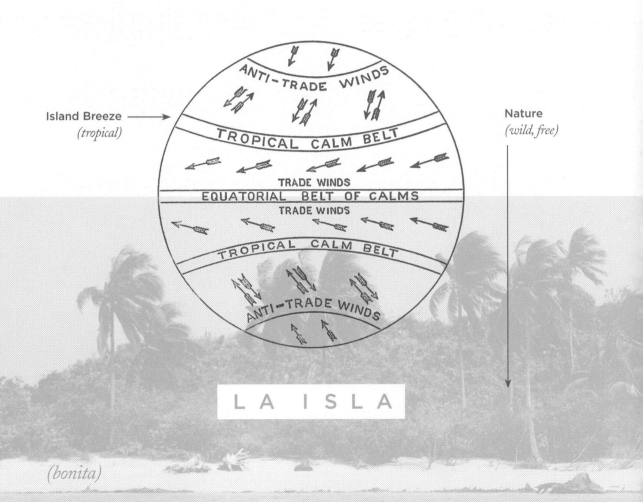

Fig. 34

Where I Long to Be

Island Breeze
(tropical)

Nature
(wild, free)

ANTI-TRADE WINDS

TROPICAL CALM BELT

TRADE WINDS

EQUATORIAL BELT OF CALMS

TRADE WINDS

TROPICAL CALM BELT

ANTI-TRADE WINDS

LA ISLA

(bonita)

Figure 34

"La Isla Bonita"

Madonna

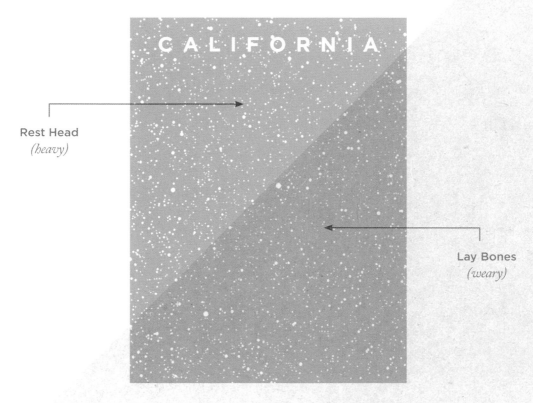

Fig. 35

What I'd Like to Do

CALIFORNIA

Rest Head
(heavy)

Lay Bones
(weary)

(B E D / S T A R S)

Figure 35

"California Stars"

Wilco

12
mountains
(misty)

6
highways
(crooked)

7
forests
(sad)

Fig. 36

Figure 36

"A Hard Rain's A-Gonna Fall"

Bob Dylan

Fig. 37

Scenario in Which I Won't Cry

Figure 37

"Stand by Me"

Ben E. King

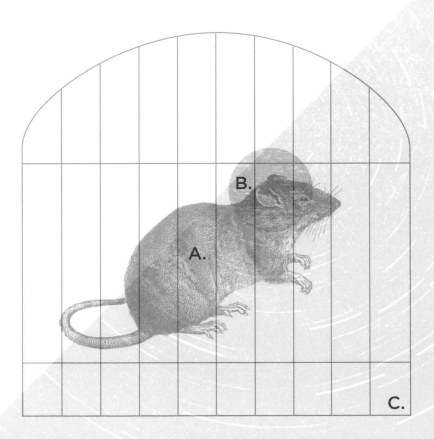

Fig. 38
What I Am
(still)

A. **Rat**
B. **Rage** *(despite)*
C. **Cage**

Figure 38

"Bullet with Butterfly Wings"

The Smashing Pumpkins

Fig. 39

Dreams You Dreamed Of

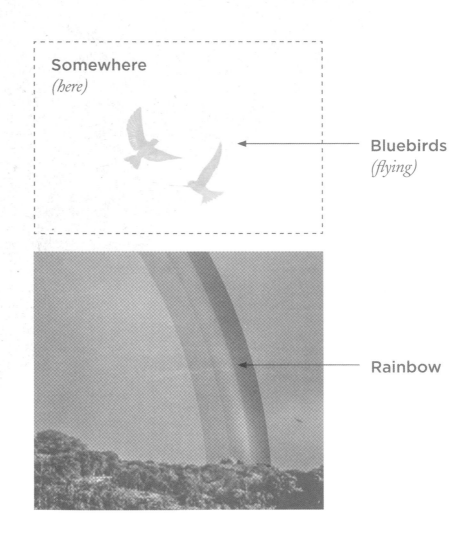

Somewhere
(here)

Bluebirds
(flying)

Rainbow

Figure 39

"Somewhere over the Rainbow"

Israel "IZ" Kamakawiwo'ole

Fig. 40

Where I Would Like to Be

(shade)

G A R D E N

Figure 40

"Octopus's Garden"

The Beatles

Fig. 41
What My Walk Has Been Like

● Sky: Grey

● Leaves: Brown *(all)*

Figure 41

"California Dreamin'"

The Mamas and the Papas

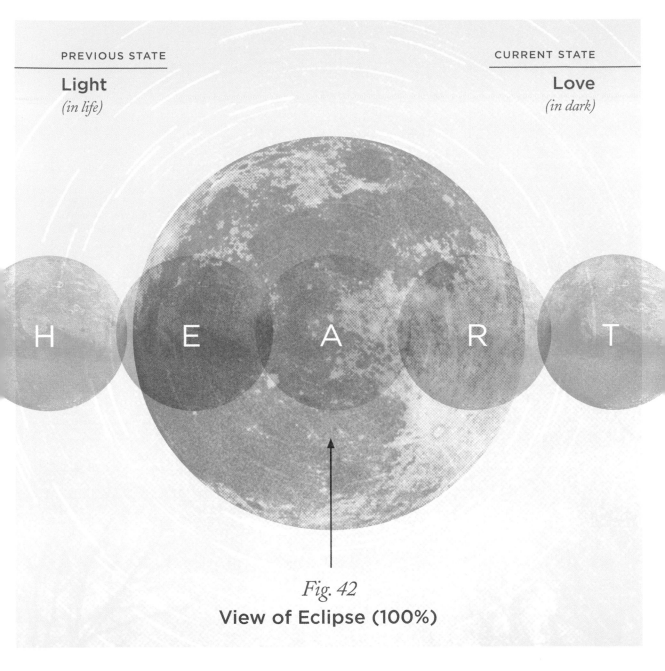

PREVIOUS STATE

Light
(in life)

CURRENT STATE

Love
(in dark)

H   E   A   R   T

Fig. 42
View of Eclipse (100%)

Figure 42

"Total Eclipse of the Heart"

Bonnie Tyler

Fig. 43

TROUBLED WATER

Figure 43

"Bridge over Troubled Water"

Simon & Garfunkel

Fig. 44

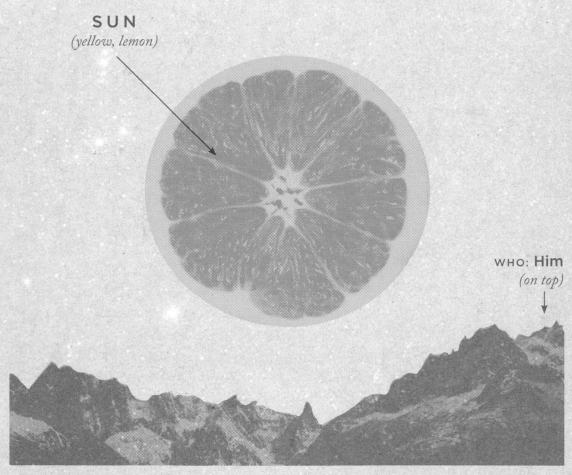

SUN
(yellow, lemon)

WHO: **Him**
(on top)

WHERE: **At Home**

WHAT: **Drawing Pictures** *(of mountain tops)*

Figure 44

"Jeremy"

Pearl Jam

Fig. 45
Que se Marchitó Como
(What it withered away like)

LA FLOR
(THE FLOWER)

Figure 45

"Como la Flor"

Selena

Fig. 46
Where I'm Sitting

DOCK
(of bay)

TIDE
(rolling away)

MORNING SUN

EVENING COMES

Figure 46

"(Sittin' On) the Dock of the Bay"
Otis Redding

Fig. 47

BREAK OF DAY
(saw)

When I wished I could fly away

Figure 47

"Don't Know Why"

Norah Jones

Fig. 48

Who Runs It

GIRLS

Figure 48

"Run the World (Girls)"

Beyoncé

Fig. 49

● **What You Are**

WIND

(pressure, constant)

Figure 49

"Wind Beneath My Wings"

Bette Midler

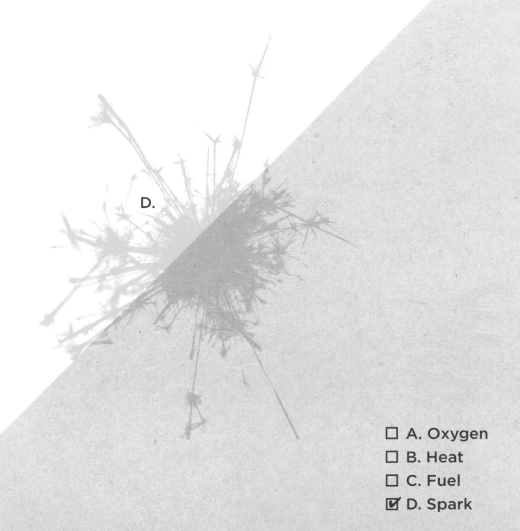

Fig. 50

What You Can't Start a Fire Without

D.

☐ A. Oxygen
☐ B. Heat
☐ C. Fuel
☑ D. Spark

Figure 50

"Dancing in the Dark"

Bruce Springsteen

Fig. 51

Your Eyes = Bluer Than

Eggs
(Robin)

Figure 51

"Diamonds & Rust"

Joan Baez

Fig. 52

What I Will Feel

WORLD = COLD

GLOW

WHEN
THINKING
OF

Subject:
☐ Not You
☑ You

Way you look:
☐ Always
☐ Sometimes
☑ Tonight

Figure 52

"The Way You Look Tonight"

Frank Sinatra

Rubber Plant
(fake)

Fig. 53

Plastic Earth
(fake)

Figure 53

"Fake Plastic Trees"

Radiohead

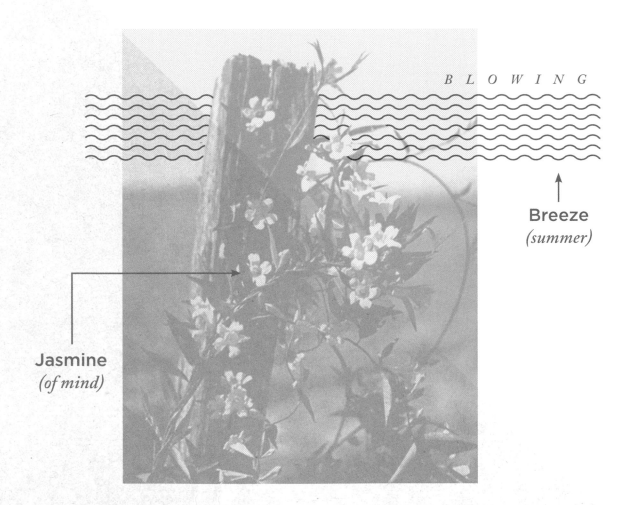

Fig. 54

What Makes Me Feel Fine

BLOWING

Breeze
(summer)

Jasmine
(of mind)

Figure 54

"Summer Breeze"

Seals & Crofts

Fig. 55

Smoke

H_2O

Figure 55

"Smoke on the Water"

Deep Purple

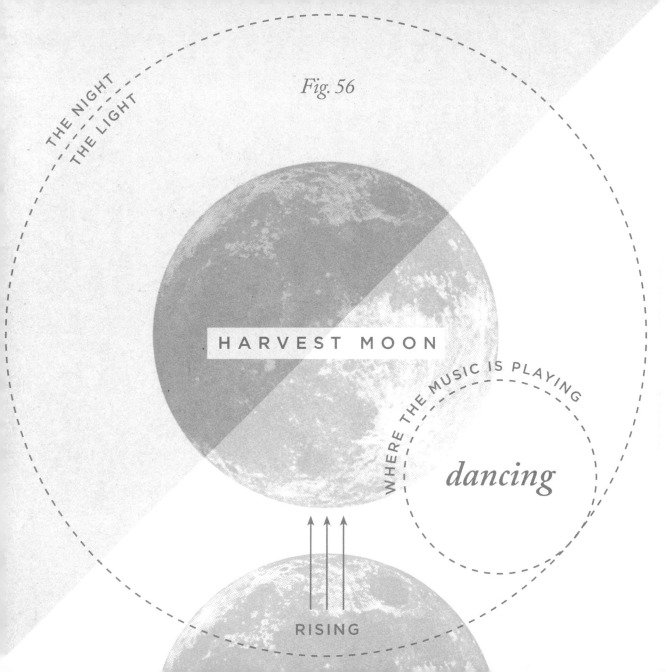

Fig. 56

THE NIGHT

THE LIGHT

HARVEST MOON

WHERE THE MUSIC IS PLAYING

dancing

RISING

Figure 56

"Harvest Moon"

Neil Young

Fig. 57
Where I Found Your Hidden Treasure

PLEASURE OVERDOSE

YOU
+
ME

SEA
(down by)

Figure 57

"Down by the Sea"

Men at Work

Fig. 58

What I'm Tellin' Y'all

Figure 58

"Sabotage"

Beastie Boys

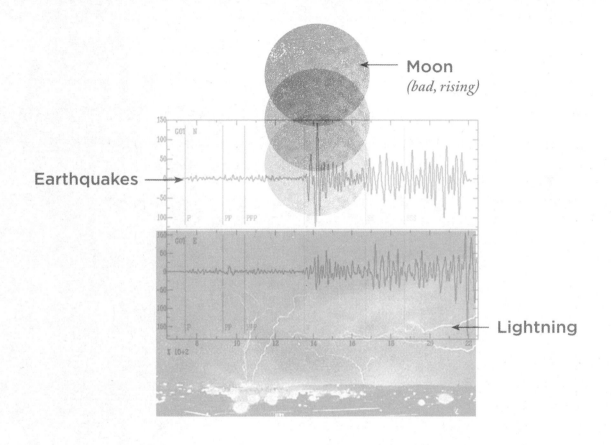

Moon
(bad, rising)

Earthquakes

Lightning

Fig. 59
What I See

Figure 59

"Bad Moon Rising"

Creedence Clearwater Revival

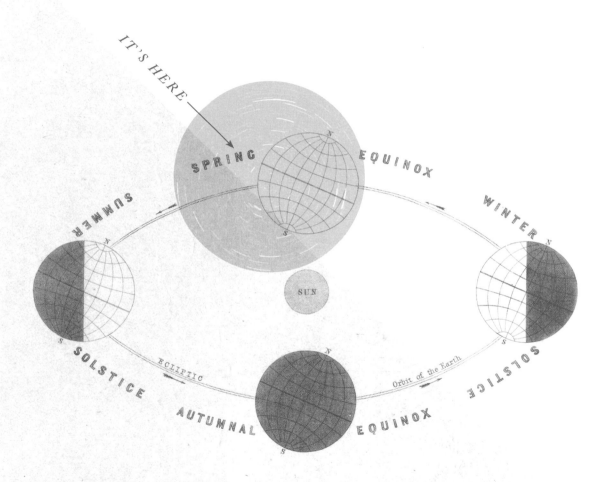

Fig. 60
When I'll Be Leaving

IT'S HERE

SPRING EQUINOX

SUMMER

WINTER

SUN

SOLSTICE

ECLIPTIC

Orbit of the Earth

SOLSTICE

AUTUMNAL EQUINOX

SEASON: FAIREST

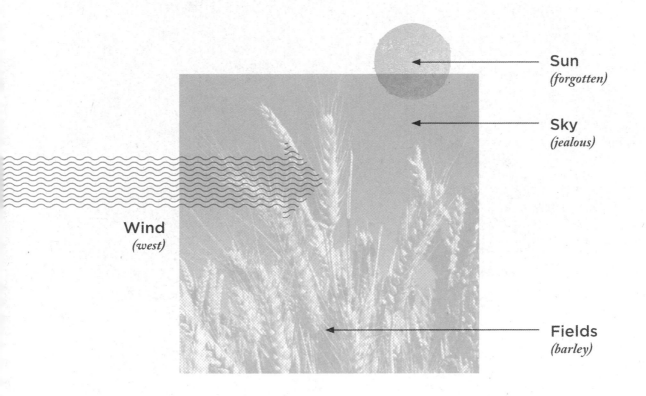

Sun
(forgotten)

Sky
(jealous)

Wind
(west)

Fields
(barley)

Fig. 61
When You'll Remember Me

Figure 61

"Fields of Gold"

Sting

Stars *(hollow sky)*

HOW
HE
RIDES

Fig. 62

Ocean Drive
(winding)

Figure 62

"Passenger"

Iggy Pop

Fig. 63
What You Cannot Change

THIS BIRD

Figure 63

"Free Bird"

Lynyrd Skynyrd

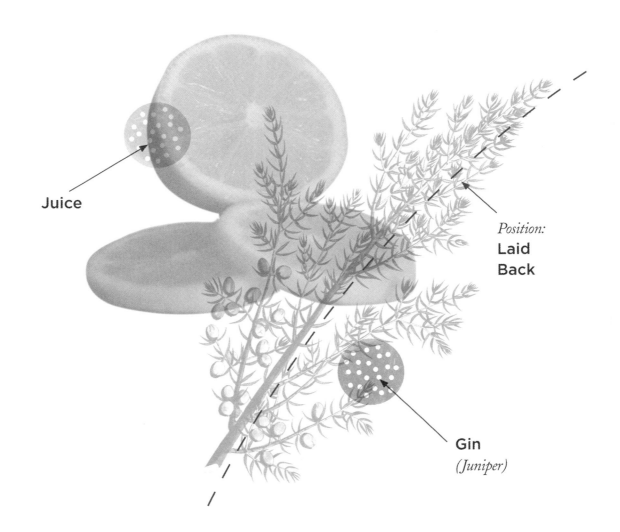

Fig. 64
Liquids I Was Sipping On

Juice

Position:
**Laid
Back**

Gin
(Juniper)

Figure 64

"Gin and Juice"

Snoop Dogg

Fig.
65

LA VAGUE
(THE WAVE)

T U
(YOU)

M O I
(ME)

L'ÎLE NUE
(THE NAKED ISLAND)

Figure 65

"Je t'aime . . . moi non plus"

Jane Birkin and Serge Gainsbourg

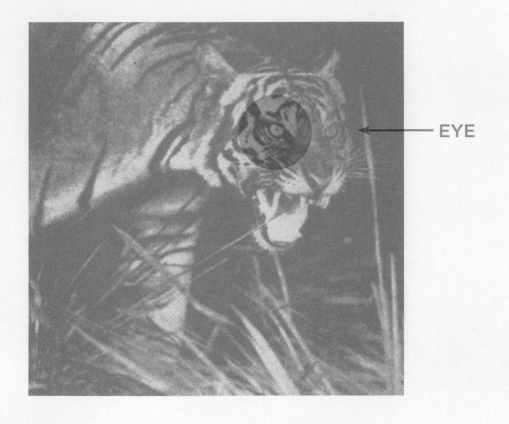

EYE

Fig. 66
What He's Watching Us All With

Figure 66

"Eye of the Tiger"

Survivor

Fig. 67

What I Want You to Do (Mama)

put guns here

Figure 67

"Knockin' on Heaven's Door"

Guns N' Roses

Fig. 68
What She's Like

Figure 68

"She's Like the Wind"

Patrick Swayze

Fig. 69
Reasons Why

THE NIGHT

LOVERS

LUST   US

(what it belongs to)

Figure 69

"Because the Night"

Patti Smith

Fig. 70
Why You Can't Resist / Avoid Her

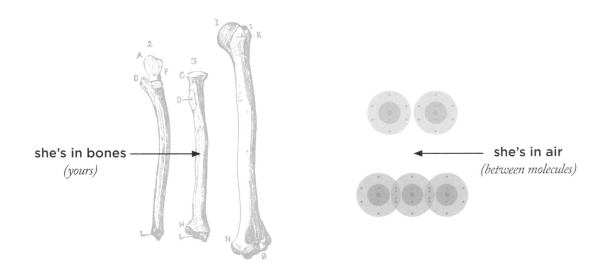

she's in bones →
(yours)

← she's in air
(between molecules)

Figure 70

"Only in Dreams"

Weezer

Hungry Like

Discord   *Rhyme*

Figure 71

"Hungry Like the Wolf"

Duran Duran

Fig. 72

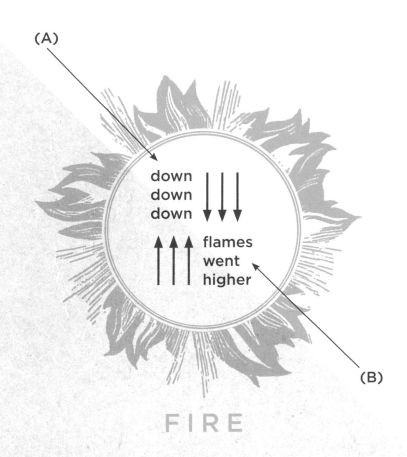

(A)

down
down
down

flames
went
higher

(B)

FIRE

A. Where I went
B. What happened

Figure 72

"Ring of Fire"

Johnny Cash

Fig. 73

Where I Want You to Fly Me

LOCATION: **Moon**   OBJECTIVE: **Play** *(among stars)*

Figure 73

"Fly Me to the Moon"

Astrud Gilberto

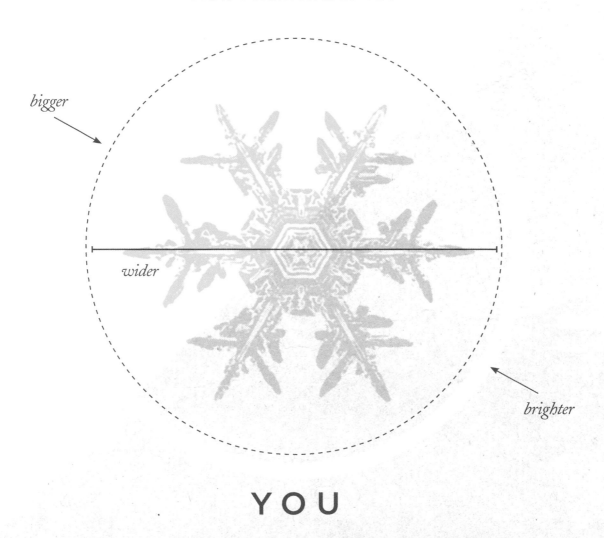

Fig. 74

How I Remember You

bigger

wider

brighter

YOU

Fig. 75 / **So It Goes**

RIVER

flowing (surely)

some things
(meant to be)

THE SEA

Figure 75

"Can't Help Falling in Love"

Elvis Presley

Fig. 76

The Love I Had Once

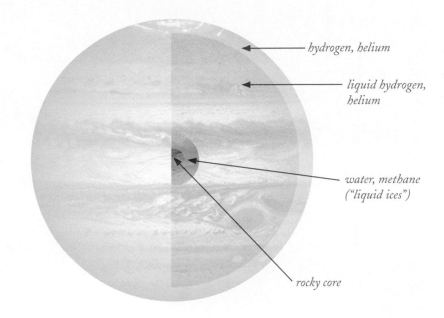

hydrogen, helium

liquid hydrogen, helium

water, methane ("liquid ices")

rocky core

A GAS

Figure 76

"Heart of Glass"

Blondie

Fig. 77
Where You Belong

wildflowers

Figure 77

"Wildflowers"

Tom Petty

Fig. 78

What It Starts With

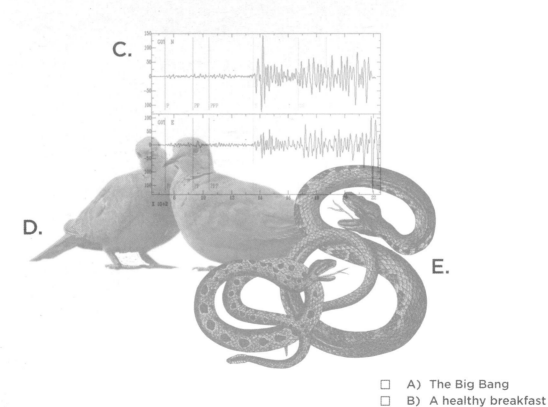

C.

D.

E.

☐ A) The Big Bang
☐ B) A healthy breakfast
☑ C) Earthquake
☑ D) Birds
☑ E) Snakes

Figure 78

**"It's the End of the World as We Know It
(And I Feel Fine)"**
R.E.M.

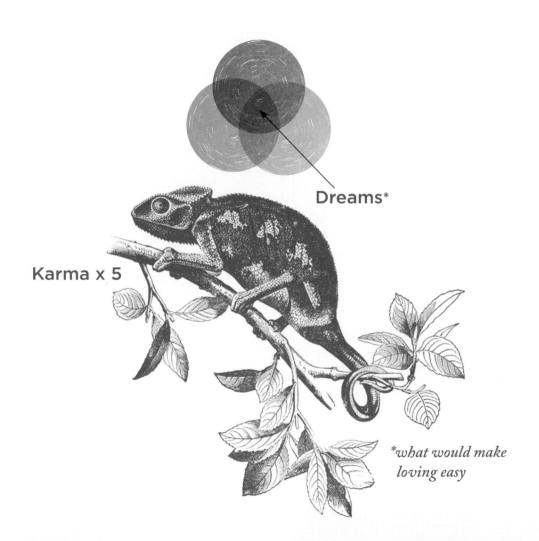

Fig. 79

What Comes and Goes x 2

Dreams*

Karma x 5

*what would make
loving easy

Figure 79

"Karma Chameleon"

Culture Club

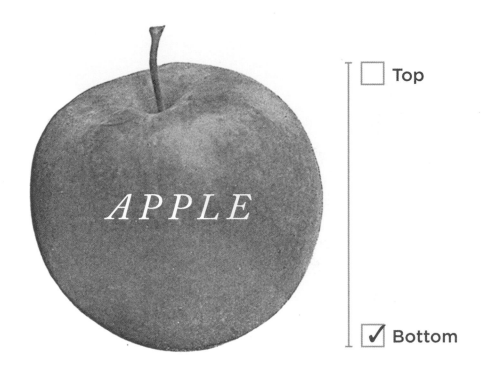

☐ Top

☑ Bottom

Fig. 80
What Jeans Shawty Had

Figure 80
"Low"
Flo Rida

Fig.
81

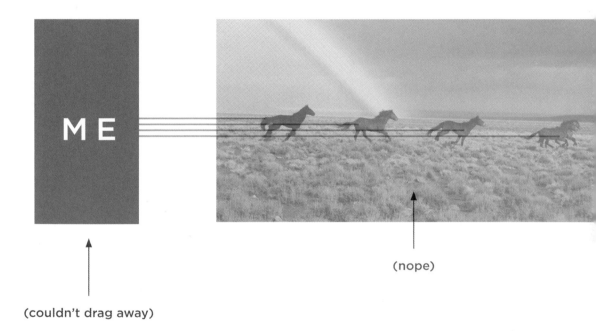

M E

(nope)

(couldn't drag away)

Figure 81

"Wild Horses"

The Rolling Stones

Fig. 82
How I'll Be Gone
(When Morning Comes)

HELL

Figure 82

"Bat Out of Hell"

Meatloaf

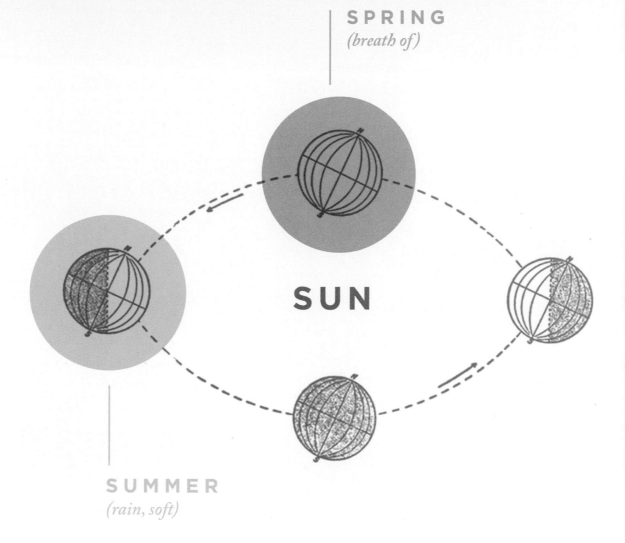

SPRING
(breath of)

SUN

SUMMER
(rain, soft)

Fig. 83

● What your smile is like
● What your voice is like

Figure 83

"Jolene"

Dolly Parton

Fig. 84

What You're Cold As

Figure 84

"Cold as Ice"

Foreigner

Fig. 85

When I Know You're Not Around

Leaves
(dead)

Ground
(dirty)

Figure 85

"Dead Leaves and the Dirty Ground"

The White Stripes

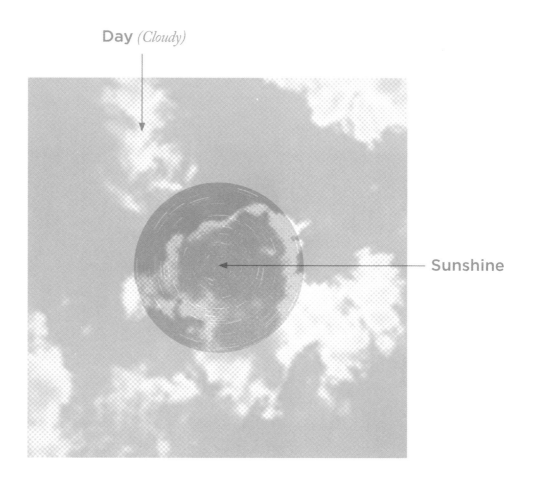

Day *(Cloudy)*

Sunshine

Fig. 86
What I've Got

Figure 86

"My Girl"

The Temptations

A. What You Are
B. Where I Want to Be

Fig.
87

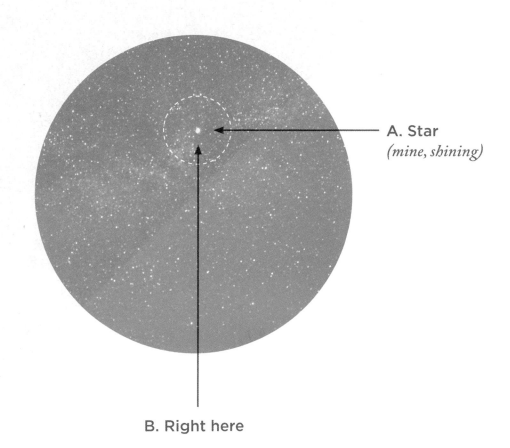

A. Star
(mine, shining)

B. Right here

Figure 87

"Shining Star"

The Manhattans

Fig. 88

What I Want to Hear You Say

this
is

Figure 88

"Hollaback Girl"

Gwen Stefani

Fig. 89

Where I Want You

(to come with me)

what
I want to
tell you

THE SEA

(OF LOVE)

Figure 89

"Sea of Love"

Phil Phillips and the Twilights

Fig. 90

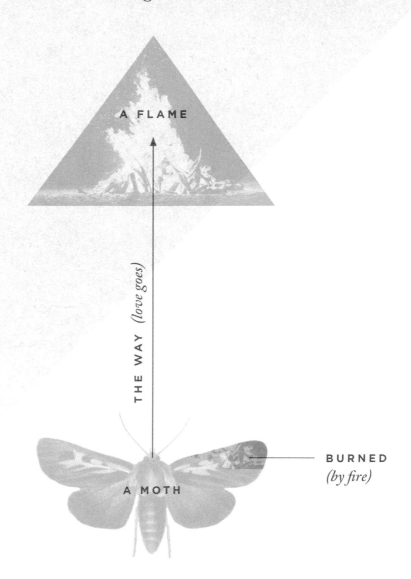

A FLAME

THE WAY *(love goes)*

A MOTH

BURNED
(by fire)

Figure 90

"That's the Way Love Goes"

Janet Jackson

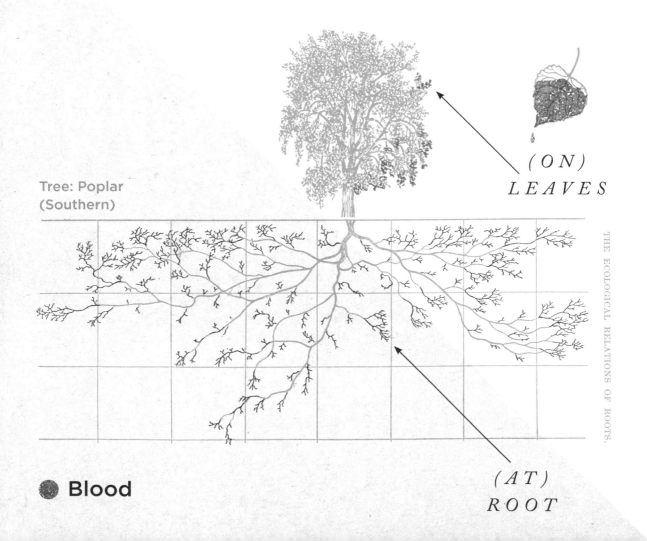

Fig. 91

Tree: Poplar
(Southern)

(ON)
LEAVES

(AT)
ROOT

● **Blood**

Figure 91

"Strange Fruit"

Billie Holiday

Fig. 92
This Morning

(sun, rising)

S O N G : S W E E T

melody pure, true

Figure 92

"Three Little Birds"

Bob Marley

Fig.
93

Moonlight

A SIGHT
that stops heart
(almost)

What you see

Figure 93

"Thriller"

Michael Jackson

Fig. 94

Seen While Waiting (for You)

In Your Eyes
(set)

In Your Side
(twist)

Figure 94

"With or Without You"

U2

Fig. 95

What Sweet Dreams Are Made Of

THIS

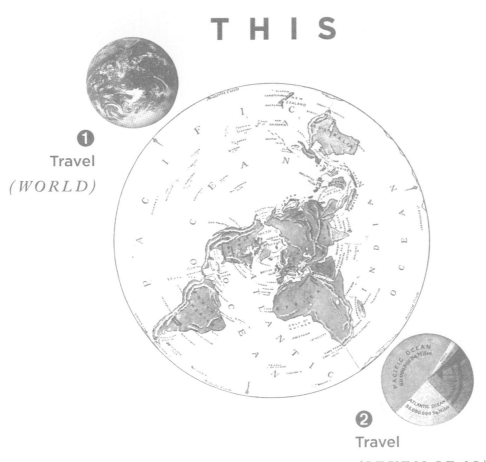

1 Travel
(WORLD)

2 Travel
(SEVEN SEAS)

Figure 95

"Sweet Dreams (Are Made of This)"

Eurythmics

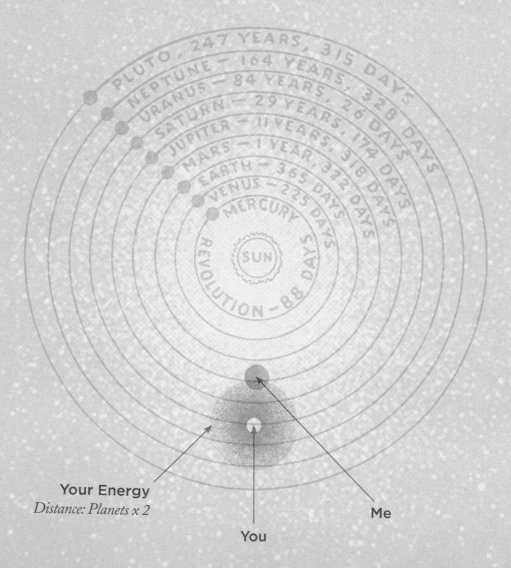

Fig. 96

What I Can Feel

PLUTO, 247 YEARS, 315 DAYS

NEPTUNE — 164 YEARS, 328 DAYS

URANUS — 84 YEARS, 26 DAYS

SATURN — 29 YEARS, 174 DAYS

JUPITER — 11 YEARS, 318 DAYS

MARS — 1 YEAR, 322 DAYS

EARTH — 365 DAYS

VENUS — 225 DAYS

MERCURY

REVOLUTION — 88 DAYS

SUN

Your Energy
Distance: Planets x 2

You

Me

Figure 96

"Bitch, Don't Kill My Vibe"

Kendrick Lamar

Fig. 97

What Is Easy*

SKY
only

ABOVE

US

BELOW

HELL
none

IMAGINING

* *if you try*

Figure 97

"Imagine"

John Lennon

Fig. 98

What You Should Let Me
Break Down for You (Again)

don't be ⟶

HARD ROCK

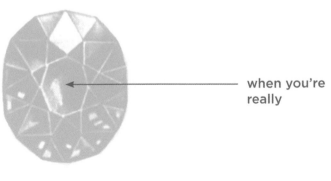

⟵ when you're
really

GEM

Figure 98

"Doo Wop (That Thing)"

Lauryn Hill

Fig. 99

What Doesn't Matter to Me (Really)

WIND (BLOWING)

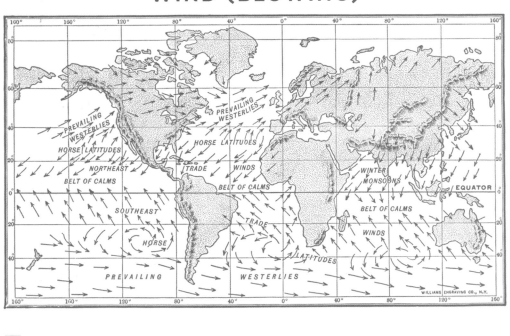

☐ **This Way**

☐ **That Way**

☑ **Any Way**
(all of the above)

Figure 99

"Bohemian Rhapsody"

Queen

Fig. 100
What Time It Is

Moon
autumn

Leaves
*falling**

WAY (MINE)

*all around

Figure 100

"Ramble On"

Led Zeppelin

List of Songs

List of Songs

Image Credits

Pixabay / https://pixabay.com/p-1650721/?-no_redirect: Fig. 76 (Jupiter).

Andrew Schmidt / Beach Sand Pattern Background / http://www.publicdomainpictures.net/view-image.php?image=119597&picture=beach-sand-pattern-background: Fig. 65 (Sand).

Skeeze / https://pixabay.com/en/bald-eagle-immature-soaring-raptor-2089796/: Fig. 49 (Eagle); https://pixabay.com/en/wild-horses-rainbow-released-feral-2239420/: Fig. 81 (Wild Horses).

Skitterphoto.com / https://www.pexels.com/photo/hard-pebbles-reflection-rock-82862/: Fig. 94 (Stone).

Abinav Thakuri / http://crowthestone.tumblr.com/image/95994626306: Fig. 01 (Rose).

tpsdave / https://pixabay.com/p-1594372/?-no_redirect: Fig. 16 (Drought).

RobVanDerMeijden / https://pixabay.com/en/rose-red-red-rose-flower-macro-2033799/: Fig. 45 (Rose 1).

Wellcome Library, London. Wellcome Images images@wellcome.ac.uk http://wellcomeimages.org / Illustrating "The atmospheric germ theory." Edinburgh Medical Journal Bennett, John Hughes, March 1868 / https://commons.wikimedia.org/wiki/File:Engravings_to_illustrate_%22The_atmospheric_germ_theory%22._Wellcome_L0004751.jpg: Fig. 07 (Dust); Twelve plant leaves with different types of margin. Chromolithograph, c. 1850. / https://commons.wikimedia.org/wiki/File:Twelve_plant_leaves_with_different_types_of_margin._Chromoli_Wellcome_V0044558.jpg: Fig. 41 (Leaves 1).

Wikilmages / https://pixabay.com/en/cassiopeia-a-cas-a-supernova-rest-11180/: Fig. 31 (Supernova).

Ylvers / https://www.pexels.com/photo/forest-fire-smoke-burning-51951/: Fig. 12 (Fire).

Licensed under Creative Commons Attribution 2.0 Generic License (CC by 2.0) (https://creativecommons.org/licenses/by/2.0/):

Eric Fischer / Diagram showing the Chief Winds of the World and the Average Rainfall (1922) From Ontario Public School Geography / https://www.flickr.com/photos/walkingsf/8180712816 / Image alterations include cropping, halftone, grayscale, and reduction of background: Fig. 08 (Wind). uwdigital collections / Plate XLIV / digital.library.wisc.edu/1711.dl/DLDecArts.AmerMedv1 / retrieved from https://commons.wikimedia.org/wiki/File:Juniperus_communis,_Common_juniper_(3543483554).jpg / Image alterations include grayscale and deletion of background: Fig. 64 (Juniper).

Eddi van W. / 09-Rain Texture #2 / http://allfreedesigns.com/rain-texture-backgrounds-download / Image alterations include halftone, grayscale, and reduction of background: Fig. 12 (Rain).

Licensed under the Copyright-only Dedication* (based on United States law) or Public Domain Certification (CCO / Public Domain License) (https://creativecommons.org/licenses/publicdomain/):

Capri23auto / https://pixabay.com/en/dove-city-pigeon-collared-bird-2636305: (Dove) Fig. 13.

www.goodfreephotos.com / The coastline and island and some of the barrier reef in Queensland Australia / https://www.goodfreephotos.com/australia/queensland/other-queensland/coastline-and-island-of-queensland-australia.jpg.php: Fig. 57 (Beach); The starry skies at Flambeau River State Forest, Wisconsin / https://www.goodfreephotos.com/united-states/wisconsin/flambeau-river-state-forest/stars-of-the-night-sky-at-flambeau-river-state-forest-wisconsin.jpg.php: (Stars) Figs. 18, 87; Illustration Antler Moth from British Entomology. Illustration by John Curtis / https://www.goodfreephotos.com/animals/bugs/illustration-of-antler-moth-from-british-entomology.jpg.php: Fig. 90 (Moth).

The Graphics Fairy / https://thegraphicsfairy.com/free-halloween-clip-art-flying-bats: Fig. 82 (Bat).

Hillebrand Steve, USFWS / alatna, Koyukuk, river, confluence, Allakaket / https://pixnio.com/nature-landscapes/river/alatna-and-koyukuk-river-confluence-near-allakaket: Cover (Bottom), Fig. 06 (River).

jarmoluk / https://pixabay.com/p-428070/?-no_redirect: Fig. 44 (Lemon).

sipa / https://pixabay.com/en/seagull-water-bird-feather-seevogel-1309720: page 6 (Seagulls).

Skitterphoto.com / https://www.pexels.com/photo/water-drop-of-water-green-ripple-48600: Fig. 07 (Droplet).

ThomasWolter / https://pixabay.com/en/autumn-leaves-leaf-transparent-1768354: Fig. 85 (Leaves).

Public Domain:

1258374 / pixabay.com / https://pixabay.com/en/banana-yellow-bunch-of-bananas-1025109: Fig. 88 (Bananas).

258817 / pixabay.com / https://pixabay.com/en/wildcat-animal-nature-cat-natural-356805/: Fig. 10 (Wildcat).

Adam & Charles Black, Sidney Hall and William Hughes / 1854, published in Edinburgh by A & C Black / flickr.com/photos/bibliodyssey/4200615160 / commons.wikimedia.org: Figs. 25 (Sun image), 60 (textbook).

Juliancolton / A wave breaking at Misquamicut Beach, Rhode Island, 6 August 2010 / https://commons.wikimedia.org/wiki/File:Wave_breaking_at_Misquamicut_Beach,_RI.JPG: Fig. 65 (Ocean).

Caetani, Michelangelo / La materia della Divina commedia di Dante Alighieri dichiarata in VI tavole da Michelangelo Caetani. Montecassino: Monaci benedettini di Montecassino. Plate IV / Cornell University: Persuasive Cartography: The PJ Mode Collection / https://commons.wikimedia.org/wiki/File:Michelangelo_Caetani,_Map_of_Hell,_1855_Cornell_CUL_PJM_1071_03.jpg: (Hell) Fig. 82.

Andrew Collins / Português: Lochearnhead / https://unsplash.com/photos/HeOU8DivaFQ / Retrieved from https://commons.wikimedia.org/wiki/File:Lochearnhead,UK.jpg: Cover (Middle), Fig. 06 (Valley).

ESA/ Hubble / Credit: Akira Fujii / M 42, Monoceros, Orion, NGC 1976, Messier 42, Canis Major, Canis Minor, Cone Nebula, NGC 2264 / Source: http://www.spacetelescope.org/images/heic0206j/ / Image alterations include cropping, halftone, grayscale, and reduction of background: Fig. 44 (Stars).

Gorgo / Valley of the Ten Peaks Canadian Rockies / https://en.wikipedia.org/wiki/Mountain#/media/File:Moraine_Lake_17092005.jpg: (Mountain) Cover (Top), Figs. 06, 44.

Dr. Donald B. MacGowan / Akaka falls Hamakua / https://commons.wikimedia.org/wiki/File:Akaka_falls_Hamakua.jpg: Fig. 02 (Waterfall).

NASA / "The Blue Marble" / nssdc.gsfc.nasa.gov/imgcat/html/object_page/a17_h_148_22727.html / Retrieved from https://commons.wikimedia.org/wiki/File:The_Earth_seen_from_Apollo_17_with_transparent_background.png / Retouching by Cody escadron delta from File:The Earth seen from Apollo 17.jpg: (Earth) Figs. 03, 48, 95.

NASA/SDO (AIA) / The Sun photographed at 304 angstroms by the Atmospheric Imaging Assembly (AIA 304) of NASA's Solar Dynamics Observatory (SDO). / sdo.gsfc.nasa.gov/assets/img/browse/2010/08/19/20100819_003221_4096_0304.jpg / Retrieved from https://commons.wikimedia.org/wiki/File:The_Sun_by_the_Atmospheric_Imaging_Assembly_of_NASA%27s_Solar_Dynamics_Observatory_-_20100819.jpg: (Sun) Figs. 04, 08, 12, 22, 26, 27, 30, 38, 46, 59, 75, 91, 96.

Pekachu / United States Geological Survey / 1906 San Francisco earthquake's seismogram recorded in Gottingen, Germany / earthquake.usgs.gov/earthquakes/events/1906calif/18april/got_seismogram.php / Retrieved from https://commons.wikimedia.org/wiki/File:1906_San_Francisco_earthquake_seismograph.png: (Earthquake) Figs. 59 , 78.

The Popular Science Monthly, 1901-1902 / Star Trails / https://archive.org/details/popularsciencemo60newy / Retrieved from https://commons.wikimedia.org/wiki/File:PSM_V60_D301_Star_trails.png: (Star Trails) Figs. 03, 04, 13, 19, 21 28, 30, 37, 38, 42, 60, 69, 79, 86, 93.

RAFOS, Graduate School of Oceanography, URI, Kingston, RI 02881/ NASA / Signal received from moored SOFAR emitters and recorded signals from float. / http://www.po.gso.uri.edu/rafos/general/sound_source/fig2.jpg / Retrieved from https://commons.wikimedia.org/wiki/File:Sound_wave_Correlation.jpg: Fig. 13 (Sound waves).

Unknown Draftsman / Diagram of a cantilever bridge, The New Student's Reference Work, v. 1, 1914, p. 267. / Retrieved from https://commons.wikimedia.org/wiki/File:NSRW_Bridge,_Cantilever.jpg: Fig. 43 (Bridge).

John E. Weaver (John Ernest), 1884-1966 / The ecological relations of roots, Carnegie Institute of Washington, 1919 / Library of Congress, https://archive.org/details/ecologicalrelati00weav / Retrieved from https://commons.wikimedia.org/wiki/File:The_ecological_relations_of_roots_(1919)_(14586833128).jpg: 91 (Roots).

Mark A. Wilson (Department of Geology, The College of Wooster) / Gabbro specimen; Rock Creek Canyon, eastern Sierra Nevada, California / https://commons.wikimedia.org/wiki/File:GabbroRockCreek1.jpg: Back Cover, Fig. 14 (Rock).

HarperCollins books may be purchased for educational, business, or sales promotional use. For information please email the Special Markets Department at SPsales@harpercollins.com.

Published in 2018 by
Harper Design
An Imprint of HarperCollins*Publishers*
195 Broadway
New York, NY 10007
Tel: (212) 207-7000
Fax: (855) 746-6023
harperdesign@harpercollins.com
www.hc.com

Distributed throughout the world by
HarperCollins Publishers
195 Broadway
New York, NY 10007

ISBN 978-0-06-274787-7

Library of Congress Control Number: 2017945068

First Printing, 2018

Printed in China

ACKNOWLEDGMENTS

A special thank-you to my husband, to my team at Flight Design Co., my agent Michelle Tessler, my editors Becca Hunt, Dani Segelbaum, Elizabeth Smith, and designers Lynne Yeamans and Nancy Leonard, my incredible advisors Betsy and Chuck Cordes, and to the dear friends and family who helped nudge me along on this adventurous and, at times, rather winding journey. You know who you are and this book truly wouldn't exist without you. Please refer to Figure 43 ("Bridge over Troubled Water").

———————————

ABOUT THE AUTHOR

Katrina McHugh is a graphic designer and cofounder of the branding studio Flight Design Co. She delights in the mystery of "things she does not really understand," a category that encompasses a great deal, including but not limited to popular song lyrics, emotions, and photosynthesis. She lives and works in San Francisco.

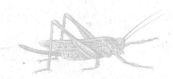